I0402322

Legitimate Ways to Make Real Money Online

Make Smart Income working online using your Smartphone, Tablet, or Laptop!

Are you looking for ways to make extra income online during your free time, from your home, while driving or anywhere you are in the world? Making passive income enables you to live the life you desire, visit places on your wish list and get free time to do *your things*. I know you would love this too!

This book contains numerous ways to make money online using your smartphone, tablet or laptop/computer. Some may make you money fast while others might need some more time. The best passive income job is the one that requires a lot of dedication and effort in the beginning; a lot of learning too.

In this eBook, you will get **20** best ways to make money online, **10** skill-specific jobs, **11** best smartphone that pays, and **10** real ways to make money from your website. In addition, there is a quick guide to setting up a website/blog. I have also included a recommendation at the end of this book that can make you up to **$10,000 per month**.

Try several opportunities until you find one or a few that suits you the best from the included lists. Then, increase the effort on this identified method to upsurge your income.

Money Making Made Easier by This "Legitimate Ways to Make Real Money Online!"

Congratulations and thanks a lot for buying this online money making guide!

Are you broke or dying of debts? Or having troubles paying your rent? Are you in need of some quick extra cash? Sometimes, we find ourselves searching for easy and fast ways to make money.

The best thing is that you can start today and make extra money online to eliminate the small financial problems that occur more often. No matter the situation in your life, this eBook will help you find a lucrative solution. You can even get a full-time income method and live the kinda life you've always wanted and deserved.

This book is a compilation of a variety of ways in which you can make money from, without leaving your home or wherever you may choose to. You can work anytime you want, even in your free time.

Good passive income is all we want! It allows you abundant freedom to do whatever you desire in life.

I honestly hope that this book will help you get a job that you don't have to work too much, but you still make some significant passive income. Diversify the sources of income if you want to be a millionaire, or at least, earn your financial freedom.

Visit my website at https://www.joshonline247.home.blog now to sign up and learn more about how you can make money online. Thank you.

Legal Notice

The author has strived to be as thorough and accurate as he could when creating this eBook. He has put all efforts to ensure that information provided herein is verified and exact. Nevertheless, because of the rapidly changing nature of the internet, he doesn't guarantee at any time that the information in this book is accurate. The publisher is not responsible for any faults, omissions or contrary interpretation of the theme. The book is not aimed for use as a source of business, accounting, legal or financial advice and all readers are advised to seek knowledge from competent specialists regarding the relevant fields.

Copyright Notice

All content contained in this eBook is secured by copyright and may not be reproduced or rebranded without the consent of the author. To enhance easy reading, you are encouraged to print this eBook. You can also use the content of this book on your website, blog, email newsletter, videos, and social media posts, as well as anywhere else you may wish.

Material Connection Disclosure

You ought to assume that the publisher and author of this eBook have an affiliate and/or another material connection with the providers of services and goods cited in this book and may (or may not) get compensation if you buy from a provider through the links provided. You should always do an intelligent research before purchasing goods or services from anyone whether offline or online.

Overview

Welcome to my guide to "Legitimate Ways to Make Real Money Online". I'm glad you downloaded this book.

This book is for you if your primary goal is to make some extra income from the comfort of your couch. You don't have to visit any working station. The technology has developed and with the growing use of smartphones, tablets and computers, many people are able to make additional income from home. Some have even left their 9-5 jobs and declared to work online to maximize their income. Do you want the same?

When you make passive income online, it allows you the financial freedom to do whatever you have ever wished with your money, visit places you wished you could, and even open your mind to the numerous legit ways that people make money from.

The best thing about these online jobs is that most of them do not require any special skills. You learn as you earn. For example, if it's a software, business or let's say lead-generation technique, you can learn as you enjoy the benefits.

However, some of the online jobs requires certain skills in specific fields; for example, web development, programming, etc. But the ones that really pays passive income are the self-employed jobs. Happily, I've specified each category in this eBook.

Some of the jobs again might need some investment, but most of them happen to be scams. Only the selected few can make you money as they claims. I would urge you to do a comprehensive research before deciding to use a dime on any money-making software or site.

It is aimed to help any person hoping to improve their revenue, especially if you have no experience in the online industry. It offers a clear, straightforward and detailed info regarding the different ways that can make you money in 2019 and beyond. Then, the author gives you several of his own discoveries that are making him good money.

According to reviewers, this book has helped them find their first legit way of making money online from their homes, while travelling, and wherever they are. If you would like to be like these people, then search no more because you will find your best solution by the time you complete reading this book.

Remember, you don't have to leave your job first, these jobs may require only some little time per day. Leave your job only after finding a truly profitable opportunity that makes you good sustainable income.

About the author

Lawrence Njane is a proud eBook author who grew up travelling, earned a bachelor's degree in Sociology and currently working in the online business world. He is experienced and loves writing since young age. He loves to be resourceful and helpful to those he meet locally and online. He is always absorbed by music, especially reggae music. He believes in and acknowledges the power and blessings of the Almighty God. He is a fan of generosity and helping those who need him with whatever he has – ideas, materials, and other things. Njane loves the greens and fruits, as well as a glass of hot coffee in the evening. He has two brothers, three sisters, one wife and one truly loved son. Currently, Njane lives in Kenya with his family and Jackie, his beloved dog pet.

TABLE OF CONTENTS

Introduction

When it comes to making money online, there are numerous ways as testified by numerous internet users. However, some of these businesses are scam and aim at wasting your time and even sometimes, leave you totally bankrupt. I'm sure you've come across such things if you have been in the online industry for some time. The Multi-Level Marketing (MLM) programs that promise huge money in a short time, without experience, only *little* investments. Be cautious. Before paying for any, make sure you do a thorough research and confirm that it is a legit company.

The next thing I would guess is that you are looking for an awesome way to make money online. This means you want to get your own financial, movement and entire life freedom. Most of the real-paying online jobs may require some initial capita but once you invest, you can be earning while you sleep. A good example is affiliate marketing, which I'll explain more shortly.

This eBook contains **20** ways to make money online, **10** skill-specific jobs, **11** best smartphone that pays, and **10** real ways to make money from your website. I have also included a recommendation in the end of this book that can make you $1000 per month. Remember you don't need a website to start earning online. But for some jobs like affiliate marketing, it's more efficient when you have one.

From 50+ online money making methods, I believe you will get one or several that suits you. you can work from anywhere you wish, like your home, RV, hotel, or anywhere you wish. Some of the jobs takes just some little time per day while others requires a lot of hard work and dedication. It's after learning a lot of the related things that you can make your dream come true.

In addition, some jobs require just your smartphone or tablet while others may me better when you have a computer or laptop. Try several methods from this book and trust me, you'll find one or a few that gives you the income you've been dreaming about.

I recommend you to read this book until the end, so that you can have an understanding of the numerous ways to make money online. Continue reading to find out what the book has for you.

20 Best Ways to Make Money Quickly Online

Here are the 20 best ways to make extra money online easily in your free time wherever you are. Most of them require no special skills to start while some may need some level of expertise. At the same time, most of these jobs require little to no money to start.

1. Doing Paid Surveys

This is where you get rewarded with some cash (or points that can be exchanged for vouchers and gift cards) for completing simple surveys. These surveys are aimed at understanding customers and target audience better for businesses to enhance their products and services. You can get $0.50 – $1.50+ for easy 5 minutes' surveys. Larger surveys may pay higher amounts of cash. Survey Junkie is a decent site that pays you for filling out easy surveys. Check out this list of the best online surveys that can help you make some extra cash fast.

2. Start a Website/Blog

If you are a social person with interest in connecting with global people and have some writing affiliation, then blogging can be the best way to make you quick cash in a short period. A great example of a blog that earns $100,000 per month is DollarSprout.com. However, creating your blog to such level of revenue may take some time, but if you have some little cash to invest for things like hosting and advertising, you can go ahead and try Bluehost or WordPress. These are great affordable and reliable tools to help you set up your website in a matter of minutes and without any special skills. Once you've set up your website, you can easily monetize it with ways like affiliate marketing, Google AdSense, among others.

3. Review apps & sites for money

In this type of job, you get paid for browsing websites as well as apps and reviewing them. I heard of UserTesting.com being a great platform that pays all kinds of people to review numerous websites. The reviews are simple and quick- around 20 minutes, and you can earn up to $10 through PayPal. Check my friend's review here.

4. Get Paid to Search the Web

Do you want to get cash for doing what you keep doing online? This is one of the best and easiest ways to make quick money online with very little efforts. Sites like Qmee.com will pay you to search in Google, Yahoo or Bing. It only requires you to install a simple add-on to your browser that provides some sponsored results together with the normal ones whenever you search something. Clicking on the Qmee sponsored results is what makes you get paid certain amounts of cash. There is no minimum when it comes to withdrawing and you can donate your cash to charity.

5. Join Clickworker.com

This website is based on internet crowd-sourcing allowing businesses to advertise their particular and scalable jobs they need to be completed fast. And we are looking for a quick way to make extra money. Join Clickworker.com and start completing tasks such as web research, data entry, form filling, among others. You choose what, where and when to work. You can withdraw your payments through PayPal. For US residents, you can also give the Amazon's Mechanical Turk a shot.

6. Review music and get paid

Are you a music lover? If yes, then you can make money by reviewing less popular artists and bands through the internet with sites like Slicethepie where anyone can join. It is not easy to build a good reputation, but you can earn up to forty euros per month. It is not a lot of cash but it's good for something you enjoy.

7. 'Get Paid To' sites

This is not very different from online surveys. Various sites pay cash and vouchers for completing simple online tasks such as surfing the web. Examples include the Swagbucks, Toluna, LeadsLeap, InboxPounds, among others.

8. Sell your used movies, games and CDs

This is another method to make you extra cash very fast. Sell all your old items that are filling your house. Before selling things like hard drives and laptops, you may want to remove all the films, songs and other data from them. You can get up to $20 per item. If you have a huge collection, you can really earn huge quick cash. Markets are available on sites like the Amazon Marketplace, MusicMagpie, Preloved, among others, which pay you immediately for your items.

9. Affiliate marketing business

This is a business where merchants pay marketers to bring sales to their products and services. If you have great online presence on social media or website/blog, this business can make you quick steady cash. you just need to sign up for an affiliate program and start promoting different services, products, memberships, and other offers from different vendors. Check our list of 50+ best affiliate networks to join in 2019. Also, learn the essentials of affiliate marketing before starting it. Remember, it is not necessarily that you must have a website. You can still use other marketing techniques such as social media and email marketing to promote your products.

10. Write and publish any niche eBook

Another way to earn you quick passive cash is publishing a well-researched eBook, such as this (The Ultimate Guide to Successful Affiliate Marketing). You can sell your eBooks on Amazon, which pays you 70% for books priced between **$2.99 - $9.99**. You can also sell them on Google Play Store and other platforms. You only need to ensure that your content is highly valuable and provides solutions to people's problems. In addition, have an attractive cover for this lucrative niche you have written about. This can promise you a good passive income for many years.

11. Purchase and trade domain names

You can purchase some domain names that represent different website addresses such as "mynewsite.net" or "joshonline247.com". There are numerous extensions that you can get on the net, including .com, .org, .blog, .co.uk, .co.ke, .net, and many more. You can get them starting with $0.99 and sell them hundreds to millions of dollars. It's not easy though, but you can still make some quick profits after exhaustive research. Find the available domains with some commercial value, buy them and list them for sale like the Sedo.com does.

12. Become an online tutor

With the modern technology, you can easily become a tutor to students through the internet. Sites like Udemy allows any person to create online courses on any topic and get paid for life time as users take them. If you want one-on-one tutoring, sign up on UK Tutors, Mytutor and Superprof. You can get £10+ per hour and it is not necessary to have high qualifications.

13. Sell your used course books

This is where you buy textbooks from students at the end of the semester/year and then sell them in the beginning of the next semester or year. The new students will be madly looking for them and willing to pay good cash. This way, you can make some quick revenues. You can sell them around the campus or online on the Amazon Marketplace.

14. Earn Money as a Freelancer

Various sites connect freelancers to clients who pay them good money for completing certain projects. These jobs may require some special skills such as writing, web development, typing, proofreading, among others. You can quickly sign up on sites like Guru, Fiverr, Freelancer, Upwork, etc. and start making extra cash. I'll talk more about skill-specific online jobs later.

15. Network Marketing

In this business, different sellers pay you some commissions (sometimes recurring) for promoting their products and referring other people to join them. Once the customers buy the products or services through your links, you get a share of revenue. However, this business doesn't guarantee you quick cash. It needs a lot of hard work and dedication, but it can really pay you great income if you use the right social media, email and SEO marketing techniques.

Seriously, you can make great money with this business and with the help of my book (The Ultimate Guide to Successful Affiliate Marketing); you can easily and quickly find your success.

16. Design and Sell Photos Online

You can capture and design photographs with a little creativity and upload them free to the relevant websites. Some examples of stock sites are Getty Images and Adobe Stock. You might need to search for the lowly saturated subjects for your images to improve your earnings.

17. Sell your Gigs on Fiverr

In the entire world, Fiverr is the biggest marketplace where people make money by selling small quick services (gigs). You can sell anything from music & video creation, writing, proofreading, website development, graphic design, among others. Fiverr has the default price set to $5 but you can include more gigs to make more money. Numerous people are earning their living through this platform. You can even resell gigs to upsurge your income. This is where you find a proficient person in any skill and offer them jobs gotten from Upwork and other sites. You can spend only $5 and end up earning $50+ for work you never did and can occur repeatedly.

18. Get Cashback When Shopping

This is another method of making and money while spending. You can make money when buying every product by getting a certain percentage of cashback, which could range from 0.5% to 10+%. The cashback websites pay you the commission they would have earned otherwise. There are numerous sites out there that are free to use and offer products from the best retailers, including Swagbucks, Top Cashback, Quidco.com and many others.

19. Invest in Online Market Trading

Nowadays, there has been increase in online market trading due to the increase of platforms that provide such services. This has made it pretty easy for anyone to engage in this business. You need to do a thorough research regarding the specific platform before deciding to invest your money there. Some platforms such as eToro.com and Plus500 offer free trial accounts where you can practice until you understand how to do it right.

However, all forex trading is accompanied by the risk of losing money. In fact, 65+% of investors lose money when trading. Therefore, make sure you can afford to take the risk before you can start investing.

Note: this content is only meant to educate and inform, rather than advice towards investment.

20. Connecting your Card to DOSH - Get $5 Free & Instantly

DOSH is a cash back app that allows you to accumulate money by linking your debit and credit cards. The connection uses encryption technology of bank-level to ensure the safety and security of your data. After downloading the app, you can go ahead, accumulate cash back, and deposit your cash into your back account. It gives rewards in pure cash. On linking your first card, you get $5. They offer a standard referral bonus of $10 per referral but may lower to $5 and rise to $15 sometimes.

Regardless of your current situation, earning more money offers you a lot of freedom in your life. You can eat whatever you want, live wherever you want, vacate where and when you want, among other benefits. To make extra cash, you just need to make one decision: To start. Go for it. Remember, the average millionaire has seven income sources, so you need to have various moneymaking ideas. Trust me, as soon as you start making some little income, you will be able to control your life and even find more chances than you could ever think of.

And if you like to make money using your skills, proceed to the next page for skill-specific online earning solutions:

10 Skill-specific Online Jobs: How to Make from Home/Anywhere Using your Skills

Supporting yourself while living fulltime in your house or RV is much easier than you might think. Especially if you have good experience in any specific skill. To do this effectively, you need to have a computer, a reliable network connection and some self-drive. In this post, I have listed ten ways to make money online from your comfort zone while utilizing your skills.

1) Website Development

For many years, Web Development has been at the peak of online jobs that guarantees payment. It keeps growing and evolving clearly indicating that it is a constant requirement for designers. The best sites that offer jobs to web developers include freelancing websites such as Freelancer, Fiverr, and Guru; they offer the best rates for web-design. You only need to ensure that you have tech capabilities, have a computer and a reliable network to work remotely.

2) Content Writing

If you are gifted in writing, content writing can give you lots of cash working just a few hours daily. This promises faster payment for work done, making it more financially rewarding compared to blog-writing. You can find various content writing agencies over the internet and apply. Examples of these are Iwriter, RightlyWritten, among others. You can build a quality content portfolio and then develop to coming up with your own agency.

3) Developing Online Courses

Besides the learning institutions, there are other numerous places where people go to study different courses. You can find any information you want on the internet. As well, many online education platforms offer high quality and insightful knowledge; this gives you the best opportunity to become a tutor. The flawless place to find such jobs is Udemy. You only need to create your particular courses and program in any field, then market them on the board and watch the learners enroll. You set your own price structure and easily coordinate everything from anywhere around the globe.

4) Proofreading and Editing

This is best for people who are often interested in detail and criticizing the work of others. It only needs you to have some premium skill level in the language of your choice, a computer, and a reliable network. Different sites pay differently for distinct skill-stages. Setting up a Fiverr account guarantees payment for each job well done and lets you set your own terms of service.

5) Graphic Design

Though it is a very competitive area, you can showcase your design talents and make a living while working remotely from anywhere. You need to establish yourself as high quality by providing high-quality photos for you to get the top rates. To let your potential customers see everything in the same place, you can host your portfolio in sites like Behance.

6) Programming

Programming is at the top of mobile jobs that really pay those who have the specific skills required. Although it's not that simple, it lets you make tons of cash irrespective of your whereabouts. You can do your projects while on the road in your RV, at your home, park, actually any location. You can start by joining Working Nomads, Guru, Fiverr, among other freelancing sites. Moreover, the way the crypto sector is developing; expert programmers can earn even bigger pay in the modern market.

7) Data Entry

Some of us are talented in a way that they can type and think fast in an ordered way. If you are one of them, then the perfect job to do from anywhere is data entry. Sometimes they are long and difficult while other times they are more relaxing and satisfying. Sigtrack and Freelancer are just some of the greatest resources for data entry jobs.

8) Translation

Nowadays, individuals and businesses are persistently in need of translators between different languages. Besides the fact that companies like Google are getting better and better with their translation programs, human translators are still the perfect choice when clients need accurate translations. For you who are fluent in another particular language, this will offer the best opportunity for you. You can work independently and earn huge cash, particularly for translating vital documents. Additionally, you can join sites such as Gengo to get a more steady revenue.

9) Customer Service

This is another job that you can do online from anywhere with just little skills. You will need to be polite, have an awesome phone etiquette and voice, and be a person of high understanding and goodwill. In every situation, people need high-quality customer and after-sales or technical service for each service or item they buy. You can choose a particular category to work on and get a decent payment for your work. A good example of sites offering these jobs is the 1800 flowers.

10) General or Language Tutoring

For any subject or category, there are various opportunities for the skilled people in any subject. This is a result of the fast-growing technology, which stimulates the demand for learning other languages and subjects. If you have good teaching skills and a reliable network connection, this offers you a chance to generate income from anywhere; especially if you are a certified teacher. You can visit websites such as UniversityTutor to learn more about this.

Those are some of the ways, which you can make money utilizing your skills right from the location of your choice.

However, working for other people is not the sole way of making money online. There are many other things you can do and make thousands of dollars through the internet. Actually,

How to create a blog fast

Welcome. Here, I'm going to show you 5 quick steps to create your first website/blog.

Setting up a blog/website can give you great revenues and free you to go anywhere you decide. The whole process is not very difficult as you may think. Especially nowadays with the increase of Content Management Systems (CMS) and Drag-&-Drop website builders, anyone can create a stunning website that converts without any programming or web design skills. What you need to do is simply:

1) Select your niche

This is the topic that you will focus your website on. Make sure it's something that you love doing or can easily get high quality content. For example, you can choose your niche to be "Save the student." Then, you can get content and guides to students to ease their lives and make them happier. At the same time, you can sell or promote things like course books, uniforms, among other things that students might need. Look for the problems that your audience is experiencing and find working solutions to them. Then and there, you will have found yourself a lucrative niche.

2) Find a good domain and host.

If you don't have one, brainstorm and come up with a good domain for your website/blog. Then, find a good web hosting company to host your website. If you don't have any website development knowledge, you can opt to host your website on sites that offers good CMS. There is a variety of them, but I would recommend try WordPress or Bluehost. These two are at the top due to their good service provision. And for WordPress, you can host a free website to see how it works.

3) Find a good theme and air your first content.

After hosting your blog/website, go ahead and start customizing it. Select an eye-catching theme if your host has some. You might want to consider a web developer to design one for you. Once you get a good one, write your first post and publish it, before sharing that page's link with your friends on social platforms.

4) Get traffic to your site.

Your site is up and running now, what next? To start monetizing your website, it's good to have good source of organic traffic. Make sure you research keywords well before writing any post to increase chances of high ranks on the Search Engine Results Pages. This increases traffic on your site.

5) Monetize your website.

The purpose of creating this website was to make money online. Therefore, you have to find different ways to use it to add some extra cash in your bank. You can sell advertising space, combine it with affiliate marketing, and make some extra money from it. Some people are even earning passive 7+ -figure income through blogging and affiliate marketing. Start your website today and find your way out.

10 Best Ways to Truly Make Money from Your Website!

To monetize your website and make passive income online, it's recommendable to test a variety of techniques and identify the ones that align with your website. It can be through selling own digital products like this one and promoting products and services from other sites, as well as referring people to membership sites such as survey sites.

Nevertheless, there are numerous ways of making money online to fit any types of websites. The secret is to keep testing and trying as many as possible, drop the ones that don't work and continue with the profitable ones. Remember, you got to be persistent and don't lost hope so fast; that's why most people fail! Keep learning and trying and you will find your success.

Below are the 12 best ways to monetize your website and maximize your income:

1. Sell advertising space

This is the most popular method of website monetization where you place ads from other sites on yours. You can get paid in different ways including Pay Per Click, Pay Per Time Frame, and Pay Per 1000 views. You can connect to advertisers yourself or use intermediaries such as Google Adsense who cuts some percentage for connecting you to advertisers. Finding advertisers is better since you get higher pays and build stronger partnerships. If you happen to advertise sales, you can make some extra income but it's not as guaranteed as normal ads. In addition, it is not advisable to buy and sell text links since Google wants backlinks to happen organically and can punish you by ranking your site lowly.

When you sell advertising space, it is advantageous in that it requires little effort and time to monetize, income is often guaranteed, and provides a great way of connecting with other people in your industry. The main disadvantage of ads is that many people know them and therefore avoid clicking them.

2. Promote products & services as an Affiliate

This is where you promote other people's products and services on your website. Each time someone buys the items through your affiliate links, you receive a certain percentage of commission. Be keen while choosing the products to promote. You need to make sure they are highly converting, affordable and helpful to your audience. You can find numerous products to promote online. Just search your idea plus the word affiliate (e.g. rental cars affiliates) on the search engines like Google. The number of results that will come out will amaze you. To foster success, you might need to use email marketing, social media and SEO marketing strategies. You can check these best affiliate networks in 2019 such as JVZoo, Amazon, etc. to find out which works for you.

Write high quality and comprehensive reviews of the products/services you are promoting. These could be food, hotels, software, books, digital products, electronics, health & fitness products, etc. Then, occasionally include your affiliate links there.

The best thing about affiliate marketing is that it allows you to make huge passive income without complicated setup or support. However, earnings are not guaranteed; it all depends on your effort and persistence.

Recommended > The Ultimate Guide to Successful Affiliate Marketing

3. Build & sell your own digital product

This is another very popular method nowadays. People are making and selling digital products all over the world. You could create a simple product such as a 30 page word document, convert it into a PDF and sell it online on platforms like Amazon Marketplace, SamCart (for checkout, upsells and affiliate program), JVZoo, among others. You can ask your audience in a survey-like post what they would like to know more about, and then drag your title and topics from their responses.

When you sell your own product, affiliates will send you traffic and help grow your business through passive income. It also helps you build your brand awareness and authority. However, this might be time consuming at times. But the rewards are worth the try!

4. Email marketing

This is a very powerful tool for building a large community and enable visitors to come back to your website repeatedly. No matter the size of your email list, you can make a lot of money in various ways, including monetized free reports, advertising your own products, direct promotions and encourage the readers to come back to your website where you earn using other methods. You can use PopUp Domination to grow your email list faster.

Ensure you send only helpful and valuable content to your subscribers so that they don't get annoyed. At the same time, you don't need to send too many emails; send them only when you have important information to share with them.

You might want to consider email service providers that provides templates to suit your need. Good examples are GetResponse, xMails, Aweber, PopUp Domination, Mailerlite, among others. But be sure to check their offers and services before settling to a decision. But I recommend xMails (check its review here). This autoresponder helps you to send unlimited emails to unlimited subscribers and automatically respond to your subscribers' messages. But note that in case the subscribers do not like your emails, they will simply opt-out.

5. Sell your services

This technique is a famous one used by many people to earn money form their sites. In most cases, people build a website with an aim of getting more clients through reaching broader audience. WordPress is a great CMS that will help you do that. Just create a new page and call it "Services." Then, include all information regarding the consultancy and other services you provide, customer testimonials and add a "Buy Now" button so that your prospect customers can easily purchase your offers. You can use Stripe or PayPal to collect payments.

Service selling is advantageous for its high conversions, profitability, easy to setup and requires pretty low capital. However, it may require a lot of time to build a community of genuine visitors & clients and sometimes it may be hard to get a customer for your services.

6. Create a job panel

This is where you allow people to post jobs on your website and your visitors apply for them. It has great earning potential and have been done by many authority websites. Small websites may totally fail due to high competition, which make it hard for them to get trustworthy and experienced workers. You can think of any jobs (such as writing, web development, typing, graphic design, etc.) and create a form for clients to fill their jobs' specifications. The ThemeForest software will help you create a great job board using their amazing collection of themes and plugins.

Advertise your job board on the spaces within your website and other places such as social media to reach more clients and freelancers. At the same time, charge a low reasonable price at the start to attract more customers, then you can raise it gradually. This can bring you a lot of passive income and increased credibility. As I have said, this business can be a bit competitive at times and therefore not suitable for small blogs.

7. Provide premium content or a membership site

The popularity of this method has been increasing over the last few years. This is where you convince people to pay for content by providing them more free helpful information. If they love your free info, they won't find it hard to pay you to give them more high quality and valuable content.

First, you should create the content to offer. Then, create a membership area where users can login to see the information you are selling. After this, engage in marketing through email, social media marketing, among others to get more customers. Include Call To Action (CTA) buttons at the bottom of every post/page encouraging the readers to look at the even better content that you are offering at a price. If they liked your post, it will be easier to convert them into customers. So, focus on creating high quality, engaging and helpful content.

You can even come up with an affiliate program to reach more people for your membership site. This will help increase traffic and sales. SamCart is reliable in providing the checkout & upsell pages, billing and affiliate program software. In addition, ThemeForest will provide you with the best theme for your site.

Providing premium content and membership sites is advantageous in that it ca be set and forgotten, more traffic due to potential affiliates, and generates you huge continued income (Tutsplus makes $90k+ monthly using it). However, it requires a lot of work and time to set up, as well as a lot of regular effort to publish more content on the site.

8. Create tutorials and promote related products & services

This is another amazing way to make money from your website. People are in need of content and that's what they are looking for when coming to your site. Therefore, create compelling content that helps the readers to solve certain problems, and then recommend relevant products and/or services through your affiliate link. Once they buy the products via your links, you will get some commission for it.

To create a good tutorial, find a product that you are using and found reliable. It certainly has to have an affiliate program. Then, write a good tutorial explaining how the tool works and how to use it maximally. You can even create videos for the tutorial to convert more easily and faster.

Tutorials are quick to create and make great content. They are good for search engines and provide you with long-term income.

9. Offer live workshops and training

This is not different from selling services. It is a way of selling live seminars, workshops and training to your site's visitors. These helps people to learn and implement from you. Most people are in need of this high quality information and are willing to pay huge prices for it. You can make money from the tickets, as well as follow-up workshops. You can also record that event and sell it on your blog as a product. Bringing other speakers and cutting 50% from their sales can make you upsurge your income.

To put on an event may be sometimes intimidating. Nonetheless, it is not that hard. You just need to book a hotel room, write an attractive blog post and send all your subscribers to that page. Then, create your slideshows and progress. Promote your event on all advertising platforms and social networks. You can hire people to run the event setup for you and use friends to reach a larger audience.

This method can generate you a lot of money if people register for your workshops. In addition, the event can be made into a product to be sold on the blog and you can be invited to speak at other people's events. All this will give you a huge sense of authority. However, the entire process can be time consuming, stressful for the beginners, and sometimes can be hard to sell.

10. Create a book

Another way to monetize your site is publishing a book. Using your blog/website, you can build your brand, connect with more people in your niche and understand what people like (and don't like) to read about. Then, you can come up with a book that's bestselling in the market. Include high quality, attractive and valuable content in the book. Once you have created your book, you can sell it on Amazon Marketplace, JVZoo, etc. and even get paid for speaking or consultancy. Then, market your book on your website, social networks, and to your email list to increase sales.

When you publish your own book, you gain a lot of authority, increase chances for consulting & other paid services, and get long-term revenue. However, it can be time and money consuming in case you hire a ghostwriter. At the same time, you may need to write many books to make huge income.

Check the opportunity flawless for you to create amazing eBooks at the end of this book.

Those are the ten best ways of website monetization. Go ahead and implement some, not just one. Choose the ones that suits you the best, use the social media, SEO and email marketing strategies to increase your traffic and upsurge your income.

I guess you have a smartphone. Do you know it can make you some extra income by completing simple tasks from home or anywhere you are? The next chapter will present some good opportunities for you.

11 Best Smartphone Apps That Pay You Real Money 2019

There has been a higher increase in the popularity of Money Making Smartphone Apps than getting paid to sites. This is literally because you can earn with these money making apps through your smartphone or desktop device. This post explains the best smartphone apps that can make you money in 2019. Follow it and start making good money ASAP!

1) CashPirate

Cashpirate is one of the most popular and favorite apps used by many people to make quick cash using their smartphone. It has been constantly among the top-most apps that really offers reliable payouts to its users. Using its extremely dated interface, you can earn $10-$50 and above per month. This app provides timely payments through PayPal with the minimum threshold being only $2.50, as well as Amazon vouchers and Bitcoins. You can earn points by completing simple quick offers such as watching videos and downloading new apps. In addition, they offer the best referral program where you get 10% of your referrals' earnings.

2) PanelPlace

PanelPlace has been one of the top most apps that really pays for simple mobile tasks. It is completely survey-based and uses surveys from popular sites such as Toluna. Its interface is pleasant and very easy to use. It notifies its users every time a new survey is available. Most of the surveys offered are pretty simple to answer and offer the best payout in the survey market. It is simple to join through their website and then sign up on your phone after registering.

3) Tapporo

Tapporo is another smartphone app that offers elite rewards and good cash. it is one of the oldest and reliable apps that really pays on the Play Store. It has been consistently used by many people making it appear on this top money-making apps' list. It is based on the web version and offers the best referral rates of $0.60 for every sign up you bring their way. This is an amazing app to make money quickly; just refer 100 people and earn $60 so fast and get paid via PayPal, mobile accessories, Amazon vouchers, etc. This is the main reason why many people love this app.

4) Tap Cash Rewards – Make Money

This is another great app to make you money in a simple way. It will pay you to sign up to free offers and download free apps & games for your phone. This app has a 5-star rating on Google Play Store and is being used by over fifty thousand people. It offers up to 15 impressive rewards including Amazon gift, PayPal Cash, Google Play Vouchers, Paysafecards, among others.

5) Make Money Earn Free Cash

This app offers great potential for earning free cash through your smartphone. It has over a million users making it one of the most popular money making app on the market. It has user ratings of 4.6 and offers numerous ways to make money such as watching videos, completing surveys and taking free trials. They allow you to cash out your rewards through PayPal cash.

6) Watch & Earn

This moneymaking app was for sale for $1 million in the late 2016. This shows the value of this app. It is a good paying smartphone app that pays users for watching videos and downloading apps. You can also get more offers and be paid upon completion. The coins earned can be easily exchanged for various rewards such as Amazon vouchers, mobile top ups, Steam vouchers, PayPal cash, among others.

7) Survey Mini

This is a survey app usable on both Android and iOS devices. It mostly works best for US residents. It pays you for visiting local places such as restaurants, local attractions, shops, etc. and answering surveys related to these locations. You just need to give your honest experience while doing the surveys. You can get rewards such as free food, discounts and points for various gift cards to use in the stores you visit.

8) MintCoins

This reliable app pays you for completing easy offers, downloading free apps and answering simple surveys. Sometimes, it can be slow to earn rewards. But it offers an awesome minimum cash out of $1 through PayPal. For each referral you drive, you earn $0.25. It is a trustworthy app to make you money while passing time.

9) Earn Money – Highest Paying App

This app is highly respected among the moneymaking apps due to its high payments. You can earn by registering to paid websites, completing free offers, answering surveys and downloading free apps. Offers are updated each day and pays a referral of $0.25. It only pays through PayPal cash and you receive your payment 24 hours after cashing out. On the Play Store, this app has a start rating of 4.3. This shows that it is a reliable app to make money from.

10) Cash Gift – Free Gift Cards

While this is not the most lucrative app of all, it is among the best apps that pays you real money for completing simple tasks in 2019. Within 3 minutes of signing up, you will receive $1, which you can cash out for an Amazon gift card and Google Play Store vouchers. You get paid to download apps and watch ads at the thresholds of $3, $5 and $10 through PayPal cash.

11) Cash For Apps

This is another good smartphone app that pays you to install apps. You can easily delete the apps you have downloaded immediately after the points has been credited. For every 300 points, you get $1. You can also exchange the points for gift cards for various stores such as Amazon, eBay, Google Play, Starbucks, Target, among others. In addition, you can upsurge your points by referring your friends to join the Cash For Apps. This app is available for Android and iOS.

Those are the best and top Money Making Smartphone Apps in 2019. It is advisable that you download most of these apps to try maximizing your earnings with quick payouts each week and month.

Head on to my top (at the time of writing this eBook) recommendation that follows.

2019 Recommendation, No Skills Required! Start Making Extra $1k+ Monthly

How would you feel when you could have the ability to create gorgeous and eye-catching eBooks, 3D Flipbooks, Reports, among other document types in a matter of minutes? Scribble is a cloud-based eBook creator software designed to help you create amazing eBooks and other documents very fast. Actually, it takes less than five minutes. At first, it might take longer to complete one eBook but after learning how it works, you will be doing it like a pro.

You don't need to have the content in this case because this software will scrap from the net and give you the best unique content. You don't even need any special skills since it is very simple to use.

Consider writing 30+ eBooks a month (at least and when you haven't dedicated much time on it) and sell each at $3(lowest). In the coming month, each book can have made about 20 sales X $3 X 30 books, you'll have earned $1,800 in that month. What if you increase the number of eBooks? And remember, you don't have to be an expert in any specific niche, like I said. Therefore, anyone can do it.

What about taking eBook creation and design gigs on sites like Fiverr, Upwork and others? When you visit these sites and search for "create eBook" jobs, you will find clients willing to pay up to $1000 per eBook and up to $150+ just to create an eBook cover. With the help of Sqribble, don't you think you can take these gigs and make quick cash? Let's say you get 10 eBook creation jobs per month (due to availability of jobs on these sites) that pay $1k each. Then you will have earned $10,000 each month. Don't you think this is huge?

In addition, you can use Sqribble to create eBooks, which you give free to your audience on your website. this could blow your email list. You give them a free eBook of something they'll like to learn, and ask them for their name and email in return. You can use this information to send promotional emails to the subscribers to make more money, or send them back to your site where you make money through other methods.

To access this software, you are only required to pay $67 one-time payment. And if you purchase it now, you can get a discount of about $20, so you pay $47, still one-time. I have reviewed this software on my website (check it here). You can also visit their sales page to see the offers yourself.

Click here to check the Sqribble Sales Page!

Conclusion & Congratulations

Thank you for buying this book and reading it to the end. I hope that you've found a lucrative opportunity to make you good money online. Visit my website https://joshonline247.home.blog for more online moneymaking methods and guides.

If you happen to get influenced by affiliate marketing and would like to understand all details about how it works, check my Ultimate Affiliate Marketing Guide.

Hit me up with any question, comment or even opportunity through the contact form on my website. I will be more than happy to respond to you as soon as possible.

You can share that lucrative way you found in this book with your friends and family to help them make some extra cash online too. Share your review about this book on Amazon. I'll be so grateful.

Thanks once more.

Warm regards,

Njane Lawrence.

https://joshonline247.home.blog

www.ingramcontent.com/pod-product-compliance
Lightning Source LLC
Chambersburg PA
CBHW030603220526
45463CB00007B/3164